Moses' Footprints

Moses' Footprints

Milorad Krystanovich

ISBN: 978-0-9570984-1-1

Copyright © The estate of Milorad Krystanovich

Cover photograph: Milorad Krystanovich

All rights reserved. No part of this work may be reproduced, stored or transmitted in any form or by any means, graphic, electronic, recorded or mechanical, without the prior written permission of the publisher.

The estate of Milorad Krystanovich has asserted his right under Section 77 of the Copyright, Designs and Patents Act 1988 to be identified as the author of this work.

First published February 2012 by:

Nine Arches Press
Great Central Studios
92 Lower Hillmorton Rd
Rugby
Warwickshire
CV21 3TF

www.ninearchespress.com

Printed in Britain by:

imprintdigital.net
Seychelles Farm,
Upton Pyne,
Exeter
EX5 5HY
www.imprintdigital.net

Moses' Footprints

Milorad Krystanovich

Nine
Arches
Press

*And thou shalt smite the rock,
and there shall come water out of it,
that the people may drink.*
Exodus 17:6

**To the memory of my mother
Smilja Krstanović
1926 – 2010**

*Mama, forgive me
for not using your native words,
my mother-tongue – the language of my grief*

*Mama, oprosti mi
for writing these English words
and believing in them, left on this sheet.*

*Mama, oprosti mi –
you listen to me but cannot understand
your son who is still in refuge in this poem.*

MILORAD KRYSTANOVICH was born in 1950 in Dalmatia, then part of the former Yugoslavia. He studied literature at Split University before becoming a teacher. In his spare time, Milorad wrote poetry in Serbo-Croat, though his real passion at the time was writing and directing plays for young people.

In the early 1990s, as the former Yugoslavia began to disintegrate and conflict engulfed the region, Milorad's family became refugees for a time. Although his parents risked the return to their home before the war ended, Milorad was sent to safety with relations in the UK. At that time, in 1992, Milorad spoke very little English. While he was still learning the language, he joined a creative writing group at the Winterborn School of Continuing Studies, at the University of Birmingham, where he began writing poetry in English. He went on to join The Cannon Poets and became a founder member of Writers Without Borders. He took part in readings and contributed to both groups' publications, becoming an active and well-respected figure within Birmingham's poetry and writing community. In 2007, Jonathan Morley called him "Birmingham's finest émigré poet". Milorad's subtle poetry demonstrates his photographic eye for fine detail and his particular observance of the natural world. His work also explored themes of longing, faith, homesickness and the trauma of war, as well as the concerns of writing between two languages and their necessary inter-relationship and tension.

Milorad's published work includes three volumes published by Writers Without Borders: *Easel and Ashes* (2000); *The Language of Wounds* (2002); and *Where Spirits Touch* (2004). Heaventree Press published the bilingual *Four Horizons / Cetiri Vidika* (2005) and, in English, *The Yasen Tree* (2007). His penultimate volume, *Improvising Memory*, was published by Nine Arches Press in 2010.

Milorad taught Croatian, Bosnian and Serbian at the Brasshouse Language Centre in Birmingham. A prolific writer, he was also the author of countless children's stories, fiction for young adults, various plays and was consultant editor of the *Collins Croatian Phrase Book* (2007).

Jim Crace wrote that "Milorad Krystanovich demonstrates superbly what can happen when a good ear, a good eye, and a good heart are applied to the challenges and opportunities of poetry".

Milorad Krystanovich was diagnosed with a brain tumour in 2009 and underwent long-term treatment. During his last months, he continued to work with his editors on this collection for as long as his health allowed, up until seven weeks before his death; drawing strength from the knowledge of its publication and continuity into the future. Milorad died in September 2011 and is buried with his family in Croatia.

Contents

Foreword   11

    Find the Title and its Address I
Find the Title and its Address   15
Moses' Basket   17
The Ink-skylark   18
The Universe of Water Drops   20
Fluidity Spirit   21
Moses' Rod   22

    Midday Flower Destiny I   27

    The Garden Catalysts
The Pond, a Garden Catalyst   39
Lilac Tree Growing in Me   42
The Pine Tree Appears to be the Beacon Tree   45
The Palm Tree Shedding Stars   48
The Olive Tree's Return to the Sea   53

    Midday Flower Destiny II   57

    Leaving the Mirror   69

    Find the Title and its Address II   81

FOREWORD

This collection of my poems written in English was brought to its final shape by bilingual thinking and the perception of my time spent in England. Its simplicity has its roots in crossing over the poetry stream.

To pass from one river-bank to the other, I had chosen Moses to lead me: his wisdom overwhelmed me from the very beginning of my literary journey. Crossing over the stream of life – the life in exile – I felt more secure listening to the music of two languages: they were combining with each other by their similarities and by their differences as well. The sound of this intertwined water slipped through my fingers and, when I poured a handful of water into the palm of my other hand, I could hear the murmur:

> *Pass a handful of water*
> *from your living palm*
> *to the bone one;*
> *make the water equal in your hands.*

Only the water could grant me this murmur – the water drops joining each other separately or together. It was an essential sensation, to feel the water, clear and transparent, while the lines from the palms of my hands looked half-purified, half-magnified.

Working on this poetry collection, daylight was sediment on the surface of the water in the glass on my night table. And I was less thirsty for my home language, my homeland.

Milorad Krystanovich,
Summer 2010.

Find the Title and its Address
I

Find the title and its Address

I.

Poetry streams down the river –
reflected in water the sun
floats upstream to you,

crossing the bridge which breathes in
its safety.
The air cannot harm you

until dusk, until night.
When you fall asleep
you have nowhere to go

apart from your need
to release your dream – the flowers
ascending through their colour.

II.

Always in the middle between
you and the beauty you seek

the mirror handles the transparency of beyond,
stranded in the form only you can stand –

the vase on the inner window-sill,
the juvenile snow on the outer.

You put yourself into the music
as time slips through your fingers.

The piano is exposed to the cone
of light more than to the snowflakes falling

on the roof of the house you're playing in:
there is no audience apart from the flowers.

III.

On today's element of February air
you release nothing but two tears of joy
and watch how the ripples quickly extend
the glimmer from your eyes. Light settles

like the reality of what could be winched up
from your memory well, rising curled
within the motion against the substantial force,
reshaping itself in the slowness of a bucket.

Whilst thirst gratifies the garden borders
where the awakening beats for another repetition,
you face different directions of rejuvenated love
and return to the depths of the flower petals.

Moses' Basket

In one of more than a thousand experiences
from the beach under my bare feet
I feel less casual to gravity:

to differentiate between stardust, grains and dust
I am barefoot in the sand
and ready for any direction mirrored by distances;

to free the original copy of tranquil air, the sea
or the isolated enclave of a boat sail,
without my sandals I go further than any absence allows;

to integrate the slow ascending sap from the pine tree
into the view of a breeze, I can only be present
by watching the pine wound releasing its amber liquid;

to escape from any sort of painter's perspectives
or from a single, inner touch of a bristle,
I expect nothing from my skin but to be a conjurer's source;

to search for stars if not for the sun in the cradle
of sunset or of sunrise, I might spare a splinter
from the other images in this galaxy of the rising sand-castles.

The Ink-skylark

I tried to learn about the bucket
full of water exposed to the sun:
not a drop could be separated or parted

from the colours of our flowerbed.
My friend brought a vase filled only with air
and placed it under the parasol of the clear sky:

our hands were empty, our shadows couldn't be emptier.

There were no surfaces, only the depth of my tears:
I didn't cry and didn't try to open her eyes
as they released this pain different from sunlight.

There were no skylarks flying, their feathers touching
in flight: I couldn't drag their song into a cage
and she neither lifted her pen nor pointed at the blue.

No reflections left the safety of our pond-mirror:
I was leaning upon this page, she too; we both had
no idea what to do with the daylight resting around us.

We travelled by taking photographs of birds.
I touched the camera:
its flashes transported me into the colour
of my girlfriend's caress.

To name my love, I fondle her breath:
a seashell, an alarm-clock and a veil of unfolding yellow –
the summer arriving in us and anchoring us to its
    destination.

To feel the afternoon's flight, we pressed lightly,
a pair of mating butterflies:
orange blossom scent remained on the warm air
in the picture of our garden stored in the album of birds.

The Universe of Water Drops

In the cold morning of my bed,
after awakening, I say a prayer:
> *The blindfold-bird cannot*
> *fly over its shadow,*
> *the wings cannot touch a cloud*
> *and the horizon is again*
> *off the brim of the ascending sky.*

As if grafted to the window-pane,
only the word "curtain" is suitable to be there:
> *I have missed the scent of the soil*
> *soaked with the summer shower,*
> *the archaeology of the rain is*
> *in the field beyond the glass*
> *and in the puddle on the outer window-sill.*

Sunlight magnifies,
I can see the surface of flames outdoors:
> *Daylight has brought the raindrops*
> *glistening at the metal bar of my gate,*
> *the line of watery jewels hanging there*
> *and turned upside down –*
> *the hope donated to the air, not to me.*

Fluidity Spirit

No constancy of leaves, branches or of a complete tree
in the view from the core of my home
and no continuity of each bird landing
or taking off from the net of shading greens;

no security for passers-by in their awareness
of the fragile evidence of time
and no certainty of sunlight
growing from the harmony of dark or in its reverse;

no clarity in designing shadows caused by a streetlamp
either in rain or in wind
and no balance between lichen and damp
perforating the composure of the fading tree bark;

no sepia tones in the pictures of sawdust
either in snow or in beauties of dew
and no barely-shifting shape of moonlight
sequencing itself through the vanishing signs of frost;

no boundaries between the impact of this ink-drop
beginning its discovery journey
and my hand belonging to the language
more than to my body – the essence of nothing
without words.

Moses' Rod

I have no books or stories for people
to follow me in this labour of wandering
about the boundaries drawn by the bleached shadows:
> *You are left alone under your family tree*
> *and the blankness of a vague presence*
> *weighs upon your fingernails*
> *before you cage your hands in your gloves.*

My bookshelves have an address
but the books are like my uprooted self,
only breath attached to the vision of this page:
> *Try to replace the poetry of memorabilia*
> *with the collection of sense tricks,*
> *the echo emerging from silence*
> *or the sound of a breeze leafing a book.*

I have no pebbles or paperweights
only a fountain-pen drawing its
essence from the opening of my well:
> *Lodged in the still-life of your clothes,*
> *you confront another ripple's design*
> *enlarging itself through the nature of water*
> *before your palm appears as empty as it is visible.*

I have no power to count the pine cones
fallen and discarded all around the rockery,
the tree is over me as if Moses were here:
> *you and I are walking towards that place*
> *which is your dream of memories*
> *to find yourself there*
> *in the company of the lost living.*

Now, I have the placement of Moses' voice
left out through this gradient of English –
the words are as close as the well is deep:
>*if you can smite stones*
>*into water drops instead of dust,*
>*the view of mountainous rocks*
>*will be clear and open like a waterfall.*

MIDDAY FLOWER DESTINY
I

Midday Flower Destiny I

I.

The curtains are on the way to
daylight longer than the window:
> *How to recycle a dream*
> *trapped in your closed eyes?*

You contemplate the flowerbed,
searching for yourself
while the membrane of frost
masters the form of outdoors.

The morning measures an attic
further than a mirror draws
reflections from the beyond-of-the-glass:
> *What is the remote response*
> *from the history of your future?*

The lesson you learn
is to breathe through the scale
of inconsolable repetition,
there is no other way to wake up.

II.

The river so small, today
no-one knows where it is:
    today
    nobody –
or in reverse
    no-one
    today –
is equal to each other.

The stream so little, a pebble
is enough to bridge the water.

III.

The gale blows the leaves
that you try to catch with your hat:
one two three
already the number of your abundance,
four five six
of the birch trees in the line
that border your way to another failure
through the park's autumn
seven eight nine
belonging to the afternoon
which gathers itself to land definitively.

The ninth is yours –
the shade of sunlight
that has been painted by dusk
from the address of yesterday.

IV.

A dewdrop patiently evaporates
from the leaf, shredded
on the trace of grass:
you are in front of the dewdrop,
it is not in front of you –
you will be disappearing first.

V.

At sunset, the sky exposes
    a distance –
    the grave of daylight.
Through the net curtain
you see your fingers
and defend the sunlight
from the emptiness of your hand.

The window of last week
    still remains filled
    with the clatter of mourning.
The evergreen of your hedge
repeats the shade of a holly tree,
the wishes of dying people echo
through the family thread to the village.

VI.

You imagine,
instead of challenging the air,
the skill
of breathing
as long as one breath follows another.

And you labour from under
the lowest brim of the sky:
>light and water
>do not wait for repetition,
>they meet you
>by the reflection of the bridge,
>engraving the illusion on the river
streaming silent as you breathe.

The blue dominates
over the flow under your feet,
it is not the veins of this southern afternoon
but your memories that warm you:
>the unreachable beach
>from the family film
>from a half-century ago
>colours your footprints by sand,
>although each were separate
>your every footstep
>had been just a part of the united track,
>walking beside the past and the future.

VII.

There is a message on your window-sill:
*May the flowers you place
in a vase filled with water
extend their stay
onto a new plain of perfume,*

*may the flowers float
through elusiveness
leaving no wake
behind their reflected colours,
no petals scattered beneath.*

VIII.

The walls,
four of them in the illusion room,
articulate not through voices
but through the echoes
divided under the direction
of 'stay-at-home'.

The echoes
    of wind blowing
through the pine branches nearby,
    of the sea meeting the repetition of light,
    of the occasional footsteps sounding
from the thin end of a cul-de-sac,
and of the gramophone that dreams of music.

Still embroidered with dusky blue,
the walls speak
    of shadows
filled with ashes and sand,
    of the silence waiting to return
to the shell of this decommissioned word.

The walls recognise the air
in the tread
    of your cigarette smoke
but cannot register you –

the reflection reaching the water's surface
of the ornamental pond.

IX.

You cannot cut a rose
and put it into a vase
and pretend to be innocent,
more innocent than the garden gate
exposing its white paint.

Burning the chopped branches
you act innocent again:
the fire embraces the dried wood,
you cannot learn about ashes
through looking at the flames.

The illumination of a lantern cannot
teach you about the night:
your shadow stretches itself –
less innocent than the streetlight's spread
that wounds the footpath.

X.

Nothing is like rainwater
sliding down the window
and reaching your window-sill.

The view of your bedroom is blurred:
neither the unclear images
    of outdoors
    or indoors
reflect your daydreams,
nor would any move
    forwards
    backwards
or even a footfall
that represents your motionless form.

The rain waters
your flower-pot outside;
you are still but not still enough
to allow sleep to enter your eyes.

XI.

Staring ahead, your eyes
take everything from there.
To give something in return

either
    the single sky
        in the plurality of clouds,
        the tree waiting
        for the signature of a storm,
    the distance hidden
        behind the first horizon,

or
>absorbed by the colours
the shadow of yourself,
>>the salty air which is
corroding the blossom
of a pine bristle in your hand,
the closeness of the waves brushing
the beach and still remaining the sea.

>The tears are brought on your behalf,
to give something in return.

XII.

Reflected in your sunglasses,
the mass of blue
with some tiny white clouds
blocks the view.

You take your sunglasses off
and watch the grey
>of the leafless beech branches
of the everyday maze of dullness
of oxygen dampened in the fog
and of ground becoming
greyish and more gravitational –
it is just a nearing impulse
you try to react to openly.

>You continue lying on the park bench
and shield your eyes with a hand's shadow
breaking the illusion
>>of watching a black-and-white film

in which a colourful hero acts.
You believe that water has
its essence in the art of watercolours,
and practise how to enter sleep
and wake from your dreams more often;
it is another temptation
you have never reached before.

XIII.

Sunshine passes through the net
of the cotton curtains
    as the brightness
of freshly-ironed cloth
    gathers itself –
a jewel belonging to no-one.

You are blind by the window,
dressed for the exhibition
    of repeated details
since it has been the last memory
taken from the lost property room.

Which is the most precious?
Now nobody can tell by the loss –

XIV.

Constantly making yesterdays
    you progress through the past:
    outdoors repeats itself-in-afternoon
    over the stones in your rockery.

    Taunted with the plain of green
    and behind a lawnmower,
    you confront your garden;
    your hat, brimless, still
    has its origin in straw.

    Not silence, but an evening train
    passing by proves
    that you belong to the indoors

    where you cannot do
    anything wrong to the air
with your last breath.

The Garden Catalysts

*Take thy rod, and cast it before Pharaoh,
and it shall become a serpent.*
Exodus 7:9

The Pond, a Garden Catalyst

I.

The remnants of a huge, old canvas are
pinned to the window-frame
to be a curtain within today;
the leaves more still than the pond,
their colour exhibited on the ground display.

II.

My sorrows have no other place to grow
but where they are:
the drops on my sunglasses neither reflect
sunshine from the table in the restaurant terrace
nor the eyes of the passers-by.

III.

The south breeze settles in the ivy branches
overgrown across the outer wall;
it is only the rhythm of stillness in opposition.
I need just one gust to hear a candle flame
blowing through the perception of space.

IV.

It is more difficult to appear than to disappear:
the niche cannot become a mirror
nor can the air help me to carry my own weight,
to pass through my self before I reach the distance –
another empty hug.

V.

Even if I begin to sing birdsong just as it is
I cannot reach the blackbird on a jasmine branch;
taken by the night
the colour of the feathers could be
gathered from the footpath.

VI.

Caressed by the veil of my breath
the shadow of a viewfinder seeks
freedom from the midday shade;
in the line of others, even the beauty of the park
flows to the bridge of uncertainty.

VII.

A lantern, lit with a simple touch,
is the limited option of my window.
My pond is not abandoned but left alone:
water cannot navigate the clouds
nor can dusk fade them.

VIII.

At the hideaway where the leaves do not fall
but turn to sawdust,
I could consult the sky,
giving me air but not sunlight:
this enigma from within.

IX.

The space between the glass and the canvas is
foreshortened within the picture-frame:
I stare not at the wall but at the painting –
where water is the origin of silence,
rooted in the surface of my pond.

Lilac Tree Growing in Me

I.

The lilac branches, hanging
from the frozen winter mist cannot
move themselves
from the stillness of eternity around me.

To know a little about the air
and to be about to breathe
is my way of playing a melody
at a performance by the stream.

A few leaves trapped in the layer of ice;
each strange in itself, the fossils
triggering the music playing
in the middle of my outdoor concert.

To tune the declensions of cold
and to listen to what the water holds –
apart from its murmurs unheard and passing
– is my way of mapping the afternoon.

II.

The lilac tree grows
between the curtains and the glass,
held in the window-sill's gentle embrace
while the white of the tree blossom glows.

As I turn the light on,
I feel how the dusk is mapping
the outline of middle spring
and how the tree flowers descend into dark.

From the grove and through the window,
the inner colour of the evening paints
my living room. I cannot give up
the silences singing through me.

Bordered not by the shore
but by waves of distance,
I call attention to the nearness
and let the air become native to my heart.

III.

Without salt the sea is only water
and I am ready for the mass
of sunlight coating the shallows:
>   kneeling on sand, I pray
>   for the distance returning to the sunset.
>   The beach is empty of footprints
>   as empty as the empty shell of my heart;

flying upon the surface of blanketed sunshine,
the seagull intent on what its wings carry:
the never-reached distance in my eyes is
the sky, hollow and evident, the only sky the lilac has.

IV.

Unlike myself, the shadow
of the line of houses can move
and accompany the street:

whatever the definitions of daylight are
I cannot send a dream
back to my sleep and see the lilac tree again;
its descending green rocking
and changing the glistering sparks in my eyes.

If nothing else, the curve of the evening sky
will fade over me on the park footpath.
The air is there to breathe in, not to become dusk:

the tree branches will be silhouetted,
until the brighter part of my candlelight
summarises its wax –
the last to be held by my hand.

At least not yet tired of darkness,
I search for a branch
where a bird will choose to land
and sing its song for me –

the voice of the blackbird's shadow is cast
on my garden-shed next to the tree.

The Pine Tree Appears to be the Beacon Tree

I.

Without mother, father and my brother,
I search for the sadness of the sea
in the beauty of the transient shallows:

a pair of sea-shells are in my pocket
while the pearl of my memory
ascends like a spirit out of my sight.

The morning masters its deception
while the boat's mast is visible
and still does not disappear below the horizon:

the pine trees will never leave the woods
to join me strolling the beach
whilst their branches mourn for three sails, far away.

II.

The colour of dry sand warms
the view of the pine woods,
my footprints appear in chains
and end easily-conceived behind me:

trailing at their own pace
the sand grains sound in two languages
and echo in as many hourglasses.

The pine tree, shot through its bark,
grows with the wound in its heartwood
while the shore inspects the pebbles
all along the curve of a bay.

I seek for the shadows of the branches
and host myself near the south face
of the tree inherited by the summer:

I will never be dressed in tree bark,
nor even count the circles
on water where a pine cone has fallen.

III.

Light is where the sky inherits
the eastern side of the pine blossom
as the shadows land on limestone:

the tree sunbathes instead of me
whilst the seagull glides the blue
without moving its wings.

To steady myself, I linger
round the rusty pier and reach
a rope around the bollard:

the still water discloses the reflection
of the boat, nothing goes away
apart from what I cannot see.

I regard the bird as an angel,
surrounded by air and mirrored
at the same time. I confess to the sea:

trying to sail my way back
to daydreams, I cover my eyes
with a feather – the reality of regret.

IV.

From cloud to cloud,
rain is already out of the west,
the clusters of the old cones
nestle in the pine branches
like underwater dancers in the sea-wind:

in the storm, looking at the tree tethered
with rusted chains.
I cannot hold on to the open window
or draw the curtains behind.

Daylight governs us
along the rainy and wintry delusion,
rather than some other
darkness that is behind us.

My footsteps pass the front door,
my breath emerges into the wild air,
my eyes' origin is in grief
before stars brought by the soul of dusk.

The Palm Tree Shedding Stars

I.

Waiting for the shape of a spirit
to come, my brother,
I look through your eyes
by which you entered the enigma
of death:

the tree bathes under the shade
of many others still growing
and spreading their green, more mysterious
than the secret of greenness.

Imploring sunlight to come closer
to my view from the river bank,
I stare at the reflection
of what once was your figure –
the world of undeleted agony:

as present as water
streaming slowly through its discovery
of the midday, my presence cleaves
your never-unifying hum,
the end that could not be nearer than it was.

II.

The seagull carries the layer
of snow on its wings
equally to me and to the tree:

I see the feathers in the air,
not the bird flying,
as fatal as last sleep
amongst the ruins of my father's memory.

I land a frail boat,
far distant and far close to the port;
how the past pours itself
from daylight into dusk.

With white in their gravity,
snowflakes miss his ripped-off roof,
one by one, they cross his window
to reach the others on the pane.

The beginning of the clouds' flow bends
over his home, his looks ascend
into the mountain of the heavy sky
he lives beneath and whose name he forgets.

Wrecked between the evening and the night,
the palm branches are not distant any more. If I say
they are like a hammock full of stars,
he hardly recognises
that my voice is that of his son.

III.

Sand and the shallows persist
not along the beach
but within my footsteps
while my sandals draw water off
from the sleepy silence of the surface:

in order to recall the words
she has forgotten,
mother stares at the empty page
of my notebook.

While her shadow is stretched
beneath the shade of the palm tree,
she looks not beyond
but from beyond to see me leaving:

in order to approve itself,
sunshine flows easily through daylight;
where are you going?
her voice is tuned like a flute's wonder.

Not knowing where the sun
commands me or what for,
I'm silent –
a handful of soil in my mouth:

She waits to hear me
through the sound of the language
she taught her son,
but my way of no return is
more never-ending than Dalmatia itself;

although she isn't blind
her eyes are like shutters tightly closed,
the string of her sight is broken
and the watery beads roll down her wrinkled face.

IV.

The streetlights begin their descent
in front of the house
empty of my family:

no-one looking out the window
can entirely save the bareness
of the garden grass outdoors.

Nobody has survived;
the war ripples lengthening
the spell flooding the streets.

Cast by the lantern light,
my shadow glides across the terrace
and darkens the stone's enigmatic plain:

to collect the stars
I shake the sky, the clear night sky
over the palm tree,

but my eyes are not open
to see the stars falling
to be gathered.

I wait for that which was long ago
and once again it can be
my destination – the tree
safer with my silhouette:

I listen to a blackbird on a branch
as regretful as a self-portrait in the mirror,
the black feathers never still enough
to be properly pictured by my eyes.

I cannot paint the air
better than the sky drawing a rainbow
for itself;
no raindrops, no sunlight,
just my daydreaming of water

and, under the tree branches with the wet leaves,
I turn my outlines into night
and my tears become the star-bringers.

The Olive Tree's Return to the Sea

I.

After leaving the sleep of the sea
sand still sails in a shell-boat:
    the faint grey shape of the shallows seeks
    my hand rippled with sunshine.

With the tenderness of a soundless presence
light approaches from the distance:
    the flash of leaf-green quietly pierces
    the blue glitter of my homeland.

II.

Reaching rain behind the window,
the rain puddled on the outer sill,
I step closer to the curtain and moor myself
like a ship in a bottle.
My gaze needs water
    but my eyes have no tears
    for the short history of my visit.

III.

Like a performer with the mask
of an ancient culture,
I stare at the dust of nightfall
washed out from an old street lamp:
    I build a smile on the window-pane
    for the raindrops sliding down the glass,
    the water, reflected and never timid,
    belongs to my face no longer.

IV.

In the listlessness of dusk
    my lamp is a boat –
    the gentle flame is already lit
    while the darkness covers the pine-tops.
I have no need to shade
    my eyes against the garden lantern;
    whilst a moth wears a sense of flight,
    the air is appropriate to its wings.

V.

From the olive grove my horizon glides
through the late winter daylight,
sunwards and along the line of early shadows
as the streetlights guide me to the promenade:
        two seashells cannot break
        the icy surface of the frozen beach;
        before I return the shells to the sea,
        the water must open to them.

Midday Flower Destiny
II

Midday Flower Destiny II

Long Before the Flowers Faded
They are true – the colours
blossoming in the vase:
>   *Scan them together
>   before they begin to fade,*
your eyes can save them –
the petals escape from their own fall.

I. *Indigo*

Touching what is touchable,
my fountain-pen releases the body of ink:
>   *May the summer at the point of sunshine
>   remain longer on your birthday card
>   than the shadows absorbing the warmth.*

>   *May a postman reach your home
>   before the reality of dust claims
>   its address on your doorstep.*
My hand bears the stillness of water
from a snow-scene buried in my memory.

II. *Beauty of Quietness*

Today the sunshine of August
becomes the nucleus of your stillness:

the motionless boat
viewed from the window
is sealed in your gaze,

the midday calm
of the surface of the sea
bears the vessel less
than your breath in the attic.

With your face in the sun,
Saturday is nowhere:
as the distance has
its purpose in your eyes,
the presence of bright colours
sail to each other.

III. *Beach Guide*

Almost blinded by the surface of the sea
you begin to stroll
along the beach with its abundance of sand,
the meaning of everything
as instant as dawn leading ahead,
yet your shadow has taken the side of patience.

The line of pine trees cannot follow
the breeze resembling itself
through the maze of green branches,
the future is only the future in your footprints,
like a point of departure
the ground sounds under your footsteps.

IV. *Unlike a Feather-duster*

Everything can be gathered
as long as there is light from the lake,
but you keep your eyes closed
and meet the images of dusk:
>   *last of the rain*
>   *the village at the foot of a mountain*
>   *the smoke dying in ashes*
>   *the infinity of distance arriving with night*
>   *all in black-and-white…*

>   *the empty outline of a lane*
>   *the darkness going deeper under the skin*
>   *as if someone is there*
>   *and has no need to breathe*
>   *the air from the photographs*
>   *all in black-and-white…*

Nowhere can be both a dry
and a wet place at the same time,
apart from your eyes
as you wipe dust from the pictures.

V. *Belief in Silences*

>   You sail down the cascades
>   of the patient garden fountain,
>   from the sunny breeze to the stillness
>   of a hidden layer of murmurs.
>   The mossy mark on the stone wall
>   and the avalanche of air wait for you.
>   *What is better than a simple summer*
>   *to substitute the angle of the south?*

You ask yourself in the moment's triumph
of slow-motion rooted in your presence.

You climb the stepladders
    overgrown with ivy
    whose dark green leaves cover
    the yellow wooden rungs,
    the shadows all around weigh heavy
    and want to pull you down.
        How come that the further out of the sky,
        the bluer grow my eyes grow?
    your voice echoes from the house
    where you have never been.

You lift a bucket from your well
        and lean it against the stone brim.
        The source cannot heal its wound
        on the surface of water inside
        whilst your heart and breath
        continue to balance each other out.
Is it possible to capture the presence
of everyone in just one person?
        your words mix indoors
        with outdoors everywhere.

Through the invasion of ephemera
you and your house survive
in the silence of others.

vi. *Trespassing*

With a map of always,
you step from the rainfall
and enter the interior of this morning:
> most of the missing
> remain like a wall painting,
> free to revisit, impossible to pass through.

Skilled in examining dimensions,
you hide your reflection
from the completeness of the mirror:
> half of your breathing embraces
> the soul of the surfaced glass,
> disunited for any imposture.

Hanging out of the window
you stare at the sky and do not
expect another celebration of clouds:
> daylight that one might sunbathe in
> belongs to the street
> and not to the hard-to-find house.

vii. *Cradle-song*

In the absence of stars
you escape to a darker side of night
and your bedside lamp is not alone:
> *With your eyes at rest*
> *you search for a treasure of snow –*
> *the white layer never tied*
> *to the sky but to the ground,*

you read first before you sleep.
> *While the curtains of snowflakes*
> *conjure a window to stare through,*
> *you look for the homely green –*
> *the softest place where the whole blue*
> *may fall and combine with the garden grass,*

you read to fall asleep.
> *You cannot take*
> *anything from your shadow,*
> *that friend of elusiveness,*
> *the typed letters on the sheet*
> *would change the colour of the snowman*
> *inhabiting the whiteness under my hand...*

Neither you nor anyone is there
to wake,
only the morning sun.

VIII. *Postcard Collector*

Your room engages the summer air
through the form of a window:
there are so many ways to send
a postcard from your holiday
but only one way to hold a fountain pen
and research daily rituals of yourself.

It starts with 'y' and rhymes with you
who may receive this thread
of ink moored in your letters:
the afternoon moves through the lithograph
of the coast in sunshine
while your greetings grow older on the paper.

Behind the shadow of your parasol
there is another silent history
of unmarked calendars:
you write and escape the balcony embrace
but cannot borrow someone's address
from the fading density of your memory.

IX. *Shore Stroller*

The long-shore gust arrives faster
than the sea rolling in waves.
While only looking at the distance
you guard the gate of daylight descending:
> *I regard your steps*
> *over the wet shingle at the water's edge*
> *but I prefer to hear you singing,*
> *your voice can deepen my song,*

it was the shallows' reach
that caught you passing by.

While the evening air prepares itself
for another phase of pounding,
you cannot master your breath
and there are no words from your mouth:
> *My music is rising up*
> *through the harmony of dusk souls,*
> *the sun settling down will not remove the horizon*
> *from the outdoors to the indoors,*

the sea wind was not early or late,
its single tone finds your ear at the right moment.
Almost merging into each other,
your footprints are the only reference to sand.

x. *Ghosting over the Beach*

Your breath
tries to be still on your lips:
    the glimpses from the shore
    flash in reverse –
    the solar flare
    before the storm begins to retreat.

The shadow of a pine tree cannot
enter the air around you:
    the view from the sea
    exposes a horizon of clouds
    like a concrete curtain
    drawing closer to the bay.

Unmovable in the damp sand,
your footprints cannot increase
the distance between themselves:
    what is the sound of one
    breathing alone?
It's the power of water
that can unite rain and waves
and dissolve the salt of your tears.

xi. *Contrasting the Resonances*

The pile of blank sheets are
your white paintings
from the corner of silence:
    yearning for labour
    the bright colours have no place
    in the winter outlines
    crystallised
    in the damp and dark evening.

A summer in a folding chair,
the shadow of your hand
owning the reality of your pen:
>   *a ghost of earth is*
>   *setting out from the flower-bed*
>   *in the garden where*
>   *the fountain water shatters*
>   *the air-emerged silhouette.*

Radiant with the sunny side
of your veranda, the south
exposes the history of its stone tiles:
>   *the addressee has gone away*
>   *and still no-one asks*
>   *how that disappearance has been*
>   *transfigured into the emptiness*
>   *as evident as a chill.*

Your face, not the summer,
filters another thin smile
in the deep harbour of the air:
>   *the veins of dusk are*
>   *already heavy through moisture*
>   *while human heartbeats*
>   *no longer exist*
>   *in the engraving of the house.*

XII. *Persuasion*

Watching the leaves flying above the tree,
you search for the security of the south:
> *deep blue will find you,*
> *the ink will trace*
> *your translation of the real*
> *while you leave the letters*
> *beneath the surface of a blank sheet,*

the bird song resonates the tapestry of today.

Animated by the distance,
your fountain-pen escapes your hand:
> *the window you stand by*
> *will hold your persuasion*
> *of seeing what is not in the sky*
> *and of discovering*
> *the south without a compass,*

the rhythm of utopia beats as distant as always.

Long After the Flowers Have Faded

The petals are there
> as they fell
> on the book of your memories:

sunshine tunes the depth
of your hands in the autumn chamber.

Leaving the Mirror

*And when she could not longer hide him,
she took an ark of bullrushes for him,
and daubed it with bitumen and pitch
and put the child therein; and she laid it
in the reeds by the river's bank.*
Exodus 2:3

Leaving the Mirror

I.

There is no safe way of being reflected in the glass-map of life,
only one way of going out in search of the soil's embrace
where, perhaps, it might be possible to mark daylight caressing
the grass growing between Moses' footprints left long ago.

Perhaps, after reaching the seabed, it would be possible to look
up at the surface of the sea from under the clear water
and hold an everlasting breath, just one before death;
or, to ignore the memory of the bridge's burden and cross

over the stream full of raindrops from a rainbow shaken by
a single hand-wave; or to head homewards and be closer
to the garden than the soft skin of a young birch can ever
be to the white of the night snow settled on Moses' fence;

or, to listen to everything a single touch echoes through,
its sound sifting out of the next world
through the reasons of the everyday machinery.

II.

The debris of a levelled hallway, where the looking-glass used
to hide dust sealed to the wall, cannot be fastened
to the footsteps scattered through the past, but a daydream
   bleeds
through a neighbouring window, set ajar, which still keeps
   the view

of the almost hospitable air uncounted by the gust's
    movement;
not the airy credits blown from a sleeper's mouth
but the air which brings the scent of earth and sunshine
    filtered
through a gardener's hands, the air which stops casting
    shadows,

the air which grows with a bird's flight, and when called
    a breeze,
progresses in the style of liberty and moves the clouds –
the sky's wounds – to open the space where only the stars are
exposed instead of the dark distance in heights.

III.

Silhouettes go in and out and play through the immortality
of candlelight, a bright spot around the lantern
remaining mirrored in the corner of an address
as a city through its outlines. The pool draws the moon

in the shape of solace, of a hill swallowed by the silence
of a mountain in the horizon. The street cannot be quieter
than the moonlit garden-shed filled with cobwebs
but the streetlights pretend to be tamed by the glimmer

from the eyes of a passer-by; and there, although dusk
never comes back in the same form of fading contours,
something is missing – the white of blank paper under
Moses' hand as he empties a little ink-bottle.

IV.

The window-sill can also be as still as a still-life,
as can a vase with the weight of water, but the curtains
cannot without the beauty of the flowers – this bunch
brought by the metaphysic of a gift and put in front of a mirror

to be doubled, to become the metaphor of balance
between the petals in blossom. They were forgotten there,
in the place of wilting in solitude, and furled, each of them
    equally
dividing twilight, dividing gravity, and with a spearing
    kind of wake

they preserve the code of human fingers rather than
the cellophane's nestle of togetherness – unable to catapult
their scent towards the living-room window where the
    curtains
draw themselves, unable to impress the cold copy of Moses.

V.

The old staircase leads upstairs or downstairs,
all the fragments of hope are just the initials carved
in the polished wooden handrail;
every letter seems impossible to read without wondering

about the nature of a tree, of the carving tree, of the woods
the tree belonged to, Moses bearing "A" and bearing "Z"
of first love between he who climbed the tree
in his childhood and his shadow; who was not afraid

to write his full name with the longing certitude of his hand.
He had cut the tree and tried to plant his smile on the
    shadow of his face
and failed, with his contour, to defeat what always comes
    after sunset.

VI.

As a cloud is waiting for the others carrying rain
the pine needles pour their deposits of dusty substance
before the morning traces the colours: the yellow of yellow
    in dew,
the beige of beige in sand, or the white of white in frost
and just a little of a green pine-bristle swinging upon
    what follows next –

the silence being silent for itself – the air entering Moses
    as he needs
his breath as he tries to ascend from wakening and
not break his sleep, trying to remember what has to be
    touched
by the transparent flame, breathing tightly as a blossom
    attaches

to its tree, charting the graph of rainwater deepening, the eyes
which escape just a dream but hold up the print of
an absolute blueness as the blinking eye changes perspectives.

VII.

Fallen free, the leaves are not what they used to be.
The tree is still there, altered with bare relativity
through the eyes of autumn. Settled in the porch of a villa,
like in a cage on the front door – the cage composed

of silver glimmers from the branches where frost enshrines
the late sun in its ellipsoid, holding everything apart from
the shade of greenness within a scanned distance's reach,
or within a daydream's capture –

going through the empty porch's view
to inherit the ritual of footsteps
for what might have been their sound in the street.

VIII.

The white net of cotton confirms itself behind the glass
or in front of the window-pane, the curtains develop
the credits of sunshine and filter what can be filtered,
knowing the window's prophecy – it is not there to reflect itself

or be added to the nature of a garden;
a garden where the beauty of a bush without roses is not
    beauty at all
but a lonely bush which turns to fog, the fog to a synagogue
for a prayer, the prayer to the music of a flute and a harp

played constantly and free from endings
and if the sky's pomegranate warms the day,
it would be easy to lean upon the sunbeams
passing between the curtains into the room

where the clatter of a typewriter's keys lasts no longer
than a thousand pine-cones dropping to the ground,
echoing like a skull patterned with butterflies,
belonging to the earth rather than to flowers.

IX.

Not seashells, not footprints but a pebble out of place,
in the sand – the dry layer cannot hide what the stone is
during the open-cast digging, through the sifting colour
    of ochre,
through the tension of the summer interlude as the beach
    fades

out of sight and, as a seagull flies, its wings try
to find each other through the same rhythm
of pollen-dust blowing from the palm tree
which would collapse without dusk and without sharing

the night with water. The pebble begins to climb to the stars,
and ascends easily, not a small flame
but rather an ash flake flying higher and higher –
the little stone laid out and dying for another one.

X.

Not listening to a waterfall or reading water in the universe
    of the air,
nor speaking with a watery tongue but writing through
a blink of tears and avoiding eye contact
with the language of rain from outdoors, in the waiting room

where pictures are exhibited to weight the place with
    perspective
and the window is not there for looking through,
where in the skies in the paintings the weather is
nicely persistent and the sun hammers its gold

in the shade of blue; in that gladness of the room
Moses casts his glare at the darkening road
where a coffin descending isn't a coffin
but an image of a wooden box,

empty in the embrace of freshly dug earth;
and there are no strings nailed to a wall,
no signs of art or drawing-lines under the paint,
only what has been taken away forever.

XI.

With the map to get home held tightly like a pillow,
experiencing what remains of voices when words are
just like swaying grasses, close to their heart of growth,
close to the outside of a gust, being in the balance with

what is missing as silence takes over every sound;
after releasing a ladybird from the curtain's wave,
there's little chance to see the insect's red
but for sure the black dots on its spread wings;

and then, the window is empty of its view,
even Moses can surface through the moment and the
    outdoors
and there are more important words
to say or write than there is air to breathe.

XII.

After the rainfall, Moses calls into the state of sleep,
and there's just the fresh air inviting the raindrops.
Hanging on tiny branches, twigs or in the grass;
    none of them
can be touched silently or be brought home

after the long journey, the nocturnal flight –
all dreams are put in order, to carry colours
through darkness all along the dawn's movements
and become as visible as anything else.

Even so, at once in awakening,
Moses is able to change the embroidery
of watermarks clustering on the pages of his diary,
stranded in the symphony of nocturnes.

XIII.

Watching the flame climbing the picture of a lake,
like a film in developing fluid – the image of a perishing
    world
disclosing itself through ashes; no more the surface of water,
no more paint or texture of canvases either from art or
    towards life.

The urgency of sunlight buried into soil; the sense of Moses
    gathering
clear watery stains or soft grey flakes begins to grow as a
    spiritual path
where all we see is their absence; whatever the painting
has contained, the ice wounds are not cold any more.

The alphabet of vapour cannot be drawn out – the waves
    will not turn up
their splashing volume; whoever has remembered the sound
of a paintbrush dropped into a paint-tin will carry away
the taintless blue and will feel the dust they return to.

XIV.

Close to each other on the lawn, four petals like one butterfly
which will never take off, never fly but fade patiently; a
    breeze, perhaps,
will find the fallen petals and blow them into Moses'
    opening hand
with an antique shade of garden green as he holds them
    together

through the wake of breezy air. The yellow of buttercup petals
might retain symmetry with the size of the horizon sun;
if the flowers could wear the fingers' caress, daylight would
still last longer than the documentary arrival of dusk.

The evening will not become an enemy of the butterfly
whose colour grades into pale, into bleak, into morrow,
into the ascending glow of a lantern –
something which remains, never completely blank.

XV.

A feather, found on a rainy day, withholds a distance and still
conducts the theme of memory with a smile between the
    candlelight
and the cradle of starlight; far from beginnings, far from
    endings,
a bird lands on the rainbow whose colours fail the sky at
    the point

of disappearing after rainfall; as far away as the passing train,
the rainwater slides without tremor into the rockery
where the soft-hitting echoes bring the repetitive sound of
    time to a standstill;
the feather, with its curve of the bird, is still where it
    cannot be drier,

fallen into the tall grass at the point of no return
to the skylark's wing; the bird, liberated from the garden
upon the hill, from the heights, is waiting motionless for
    another motion
as the rainbow anchors its raindrops, the morning as patient

as a cloud lengthening itself. Moses' gaze tries
to choose the fruit most appropriate for a still-life;
as long as he holds his stare at the rainbow sunbathing
    its arch,
the fruit keeps its outer stillness more persistently than its
    inner quietness;

as sufficient as the pain of everywhere,
daylight is filtered through the feather
which cannot be doubled or multiplied by that
which was once the glass of Moses' geometric mirror.

FIND THE TITLE AND ITS ADDRESS
II

Find the Title and its Address II

I.

You need a bridge to cross over
a stream
to gaze at the reflection
that the water
conjures of being passable:

a marble grasp on your reason
can detonate the blue
empty of clouds,
full of sifting colours funnelled to noon
through your closed eyes, under the seam.

You and the river-bank opposite
are apart from each other,
staring at the horizon –
the sheet of metallic distance
sounds like thunder:

a stone cradled in your palm
has the power
of the shadow weight;
of leaving and not returning to the air –
the element independent of gravity.

II.

Places are always somewhere else,
never in the traces marked with footprints:
a compass cannot help in the search

for a shaft of light from a kitchen,
a shaft without leaving,
without take off, without landing,

only the sound of tap-water dripping
into a sink, the sound which echoes
like a bird, in fear, flying backwards.

Even an entire destination can be reached
by the firm cone of your torchlight
as the flock of your breath touches

its airy nest without peace, without security:
there is no foundation stone for the centre of a family,
only gravel under your feet as if you enter

the season of elsewhere, a common verb
lasting longer than its infinitive, prayer –
a defensive weapon against yourself

as you silence a silence
or dust
in the stone of a doorstep.

III.

By the wall, the lantern gives
the only light which belongs
to the house in the dark
while you walk beside the fence, the hedge:

it's easy to pass by the lantern's glow
but the evening halts your pace:
the street lights fail to mediate
between your shadow and that of the house.

There is no passer-by to decipher
the murmur from the garden fountain,
you cannot see the ritual of stars
gathered beyond the accumulative sky:

what could the night miss, if you stay
where you are, in the danger of itself?
Find the address before rainwater settles
like vapour in your upturned hat.